HEROES
OF THE US MILITARY

HEROES OF THE
US MARINES

By Maria Nelson

Gareth Stevens
Publishing

Please visit our website, www.garethstevens.com. For a free color catalog of all our high-quality books, call toll free 1-800-542-2595 or fax 1-877-542-2596.

Library of Congress Cataloging-in-Publication Data

Nelson, Maria.
Heroes of the US Marines / Maria Nelson.
    p. cm. — (Heroes of the US military)
Includes index.
ISBN 978-1-4339-7245-4 (pbk.)
ISBN 978-1-4339-7246-1 (6-pack)
ISBN 978-1-4339-7244-7 (library binding)
1. United States. Marine Corps—Juvenile literature. 2. Marines—United States—Juvenile literature. I. Title.
VE23.N46 2013
359.9'60973—dc23

                                            2011051635

First Edition

Published in 2013 by
Gareth Stevens Publishing
111 East 14th Street, Suite 349
New York, NY 10003

Designer: Michael J. Flynn
Editor: Therese Shea

Photo credits: Cover, p. 1 MILpictures by Tom Weber/The Image Bank/Getty Images; courtesy of US Marines: p. 4 by Lance Cpl. Daniel A. Wetzel, 5, 9, 16, 22–23 by Pfc. C. Warren Peace, 25, 26 by Lance Cpl. Christine A. Shifflet, 28, 28–29 by US Army Sgt. Daniel Lucas; pp. 6–7, 21 MPI/Archive Photos/Getty Images; p. 8 Archive Photos/Getty Images; courtesy of US Navy p. 10; p. 11 Lexington Herald-Leader/ McClatchy-Tribune/Getty Images; p. 12 OneSmallSquare/Shutterstock.com; p. 13 JustASC/ Shutterstock.com; p. 14 Pictorial Parade/Archive Photos/Getty Images; p. 15 Buyenlarge/ Archive Photos/Getty Images; p. 17 Michael G. Smith/Shutterstock.com; p. 18 FPG/Archive Photos/ Getty Images; p. 19 Al Fenn/Time & Life Pictures/Getty Images; p. 27 Ron Galella, Ltd./Wire Image/ Getty Images; p. 28 Keith McIntyre/Shutterstock.com.

Printed in the United States of America

CPSIA compliance information: Batch #CS12GS: For further information contact Gareth Stevens, New York, New York at 1-800-542-2595.

CONTENTS

Words in the glossary appear in **bold** type the first time they are used in the text.

THE BRAVE MARINES

In 2009, Dakota Meyer made a choice that saved more than 30 lives. Meyer, at that time an infantry corporal in the US Marine **Corps** (USMC), was traveling with Afghan and American soldiers in Afghanistan. The group was attacked by the Taliban **terrorist** group while Meyer and another soldier were just a short distance away. Meyer heard their calls for help, but officers told him to stay back. Against orders, Meyer and another marine rushed in. For 6 hours, they fought the Taliban and rescued wounded soldiers.

Marines are often a key part of dangerous **missions** around the world. Many prove to be true heroes like Dakota Meyer.

In September 2011, President Obama awarded Dakota Meyer the Medal of Honor for his bravery.

4

Archibald Henderson

Colonel Archibald Henderson became the fifth USMC commandant when he was 37 years old.

The Marine Commandant

The highest-ranking officer of the USMC is the commandant. He's responsible for the whole corps, which means he often has to make difficult decisions. Archibald Henderson held the position of commandant from 1820 to 1859, the longest stretch in USMC history. Unlike many high-ranking officers, Henderson continued to fight alongside his marines while he was commandant.

EARLY MARINE CORPS HISTORY

The US Marine Corps dates back to the birth of the United States. Marine forces were formed in 1775 to serve with the US Navy during the American Revolution. They took part in many deadly operations, both ship-to-ship and on shore.

The marines called the castle they captured during the Battle of Chapultepec "the Halls of Montezuma." The castle and event are remembered in the first line of "The Marines' Hymn," their official song.

During the Mexican-American War (1846–1848), the marines began to set themselves apart as one of the best military forces in the world. In 1847, the marines captured an important Mexican stronghold during the Battle of Chapultepec. They fought fiercely for 2 days until they were able to raise the US flag, the signal of their victory.

Semper Fi

The Marine Corps saying, or motto, is *Semper Fidelis*, which is Latin for "always faithful." Marines often shorten this to *Semper Fi*. However, until 1871, the USMC motto was "First to Fight." This saying still applies as the marines often fight on the front lines.

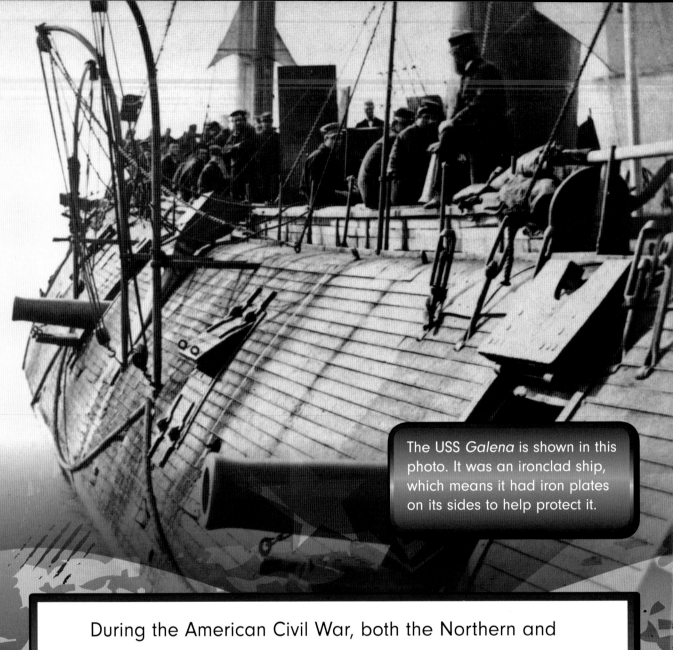

The USS *Galena* is shown in this photo. It was an ironclad ship, which means it had iron plates on its sides to help protect it.

During the American Civil War, both the Northern and Southern military forces included a marine corps. Seventeen US marines were honored for their bravery during the war, including Corporal John Mackie. During the 1862 Battle of Drewry's Bluff in Virginia, Mackie served on the USS *Galena*. He fearlessly maintained gun operations though fellow soldiers around him were killed.

Like the courageous Mackie, many marines today risk their lives to protect US citizens and others all over the world. No longer part of the US Navy, the USMC is its own branch of the military. However, marines work closely with the army, navy, and air force during large missions.

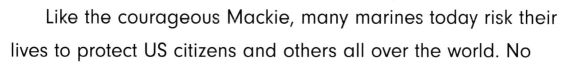

John Mackie

The Rifleman's Creed

All marine recruits are required to learn "The Rifleman's Creed." A creed is a statement of belief. This creed is thought to have been written during World War II. It states that a marine's rifle is part of him. Together they serve to defend the country "until victory is America's and there is no enemy."

THE MEDAL OF HONOR

US marines practice three values as they fight for the United States all over the world: honor, commitment, and courage. The highest award for courage in the US military is the Medal of Honor. The army and air force each have a Medal of Honor. The navy, marines, and coast guard share a Medal of Honor. Corporal John Mackie was the first marine to earn this honor.

Some marines have received the Medal of Honor twice. Major Louis Cukela fought overseas in World War I. For his courageous actions, including crossing German lines during heavy gunfire, he earned both an army and a navy Medal of Honor.

In 1918, Major Louis Cukela single-handedly killed an enemy machine-gun crew and captured four enemy soldiers and two more guns.

The figure on the right of the Medal of Honor is Minerva, the Roman goddess of war and wisdom. She is battling an enemy with snakes in his hand, called Discord.

The Medal of Honor by the Numbers

(as of January 2012)

Year the Medal of Honor was created: 1861

Number of marines who have received the Medal of Honor: 297

Number of two-time Medal of Honor winners: 19

Number of female Medal of Honor winners: 1

MORE MILITARY DECORATIONS

In addition to the Medal of Honor, many different awards, or decorations, may be presented to marines for their actions. After the Medal of Honor, the Navy Cross is the second-highest medal awarded for heroism in battle. The Silver Star is the next highest. Both of these decorations honor those who perform beyond what's expected of them.

The Purple Heart is given to those who are hurt or killed by enemies in battle. Many marines have received the Purple Heart while recovering from their wounds. However, because some lose their lives earning it, the award is often given to a marine's family.

The Purple Heart is the oldest US military medal. Its creator, George Washington, is pictured on it.

You can tell the ranks of USMC soldiers by the patch on the upper sleeves of their coat.

Dress Blues

Marines look striking when wearing their "dress blues." This formal uniform includes a dark blue coat, light blue pants, black shoes, white gloves, and a white hat. Marines who have won awards display them on their coat. They wear medals on the left side of the chest and ribbons on the right.

THE DEVIL DOGS OF WORLD WAR I

During World War I, German forces held Belleau Wood outside Paris, France. In June 1918, US forces approached from an open meadow, suffering great losses due to hidden German machine guns. However, once the marines reached the woods, they found protection among the trees. Marine **snipers** took out the machine gunners while others fought in hand-to-hand **combat**.

The French changed their name for the wood, *Bois Belleau*, to *Bois de la Brigade de Marine* to honor the Marine Corps.

The marines lost more men during the Battle of Belleau Wood than in any previous battle. But after 20 days of fighting, they controlled the area. US General John J. Pershing praised the marines, saying, "The deadliest weapon in the world is a marine and his rifle."

The marines used their German nickname on materials such as this poster to attract new recruits.

Devil Dogs

German forces are said to have admired the marines' skills and endurance as they fought in Belleau Wood. They called the marines *Teufel Hunden*, or "devil dogs." This name highlights the fierceness of marines in a combat situation.

A HERO OF WORLD WAR II

Sergeant John Basilone was the first marine awarded the Medal of Honor during World War II. He became a national hero, appearing in magazines and touring the United States to gain financial support for the war. However, Basilone chose to return to action instead of staying home to enjoy the fame and glory.

Basilone took part in one of the most famous battles in USMC history—the US attack on the Japanese island of Iwo Jima in 1945. He destroyed an enemy stronghold by himself and helped free a tank, both during heavy gunfire. But US **casualties** were great on Iwo Jima, and Basilone was one of those who died.

John Basilone earned a Navy Cross for his brave actions on Iwo Jima.

USMC War Memorial

The USMC War Memorial shows a proud moment in Marine Corps history—the victorious raising of the US flag on Iwo Jima. Though this moment took place during World War II, the memorial honors all the heroic marines who have served since 1775. The USMC War Memorial is in Virginia along the northern edge of Arlington National Cemetery.

The memorial was created from a photograph taken on Iwo Jima on February 23, 1945.

USMC ATHLETES

Some USMC heroes are athletes. Ted Williams was an outfielder for the Boston Red Sox when he was **drafted** in 1942. He became a marine pilot but didn't see combat until the **Korean War**. Williams flew 49 combat missions in 1953.

Eddie LaBaron, former quarterback for the Washington Redskins and the Dallas Cowboys, fought in the Korean War as a US marine. He earned a Bronze Star for his leadership and bravery. Famous Pittsburgh Pirates outfielder Roberto Clemente joined the marines in 1958, during his baseball career, and served until 1964.

Ted Williams missed almost five full seasons of baseball because of his duties as a marine. He still earned 521 home runs over his career.

In 1964, Billy Mills set a then–Olympic record for running 10,000 meters (6.2 miles) in 28 minutes 24.4 seconds.

Marine Olympians

US marines perform missions that require incredible physical fitness. Perhaps it's not surprising that they've represented the United States as Olympic athletes. In 1964, Billy Mills, an officer in the USMC, won a gold medal after running 10,000 meters (6.2 miles) in the Olympics. Mills is the only American to have won that event.

A MARINE IN SPACE

Many US marines have shown their bravery beyond the battlefield—and some even beyond Earth! John Glenn earned the Congressional Space Medal of Honor and many other decorations as one of these famous marine astronauts.

Glenn joined the USMC in 1943 as a fighter pilot. During World War II, he flew 59 combat missions. During the Korean War, he flew 63 combat missions for the marines and an additional 27 as a pilot for the air force. Glenn began working with the National Aeronautics and Space Administration (NASA) in 1959. In 1962, he piloted the first manned US spacecraft to orbit Earth.

Hero of the Vietnam War

Colonel John Ripley earned his first of many decorations, a Navy Cross, during the **Vietnam War.** In 1972, Ripley held off North Vietnamese forces by placing explosives beneath the Dong Ha Bridge. He used his teeth to attach the fuses to the explosives.

Not only was John Glenn a combat pilot and an astronaut, he was also a US senator from 1974 to 1999.

FEMALE MARINES

Women cannot be assigned to ground combat positions in the US military. However, many heroic women have served in USMC support positions since 1918. That year, Opha Mae Johnson became the first female marine.

Lance Corporal Christina Humphrey is pictured here with her Purple Heart. She was a member of a Female Search Force in Iraq.

In 2005, Lance Corporal Christina Humphrey received the Purple Heart for injuries after a bomber attacked a group of trucks near Iraq. When her truck tipped over, Humphrey hurt her back and was badly burned. She survived the bombing and the gunfire that followed. However, three of her fellow female marines didn't survive. They were the first female marines to die in the Iraq war.

Heroes in Training

Training to become a marine is physically and mentally challenging. Marines must be fit and determined in order to complete the tough 12 weeks of boot camp—and that's just the beginning! Marine recruits train to march long distances and use firearms. Some learn more specialized skills such as sniping, speaking other languages, and reconnaissance.

MARINES IN RECENT COMBAT

Today, the USMC is often the "first to fight," just like their motto said. When the US military entered Iraq in 2003, marines fought in some of the deadliest battles of the war.

In April 2004, Corporal Jason Dunham was leading a reconnaissance mission near Karabilah, Iraq. Gunshots sounded nearby, and his group moved toward them. As they tried to stop a group of **insurgents** from leaving the scene, one of them attacked Dunham and threw a small bomb. Dunham covered it with his helmet, taking the whole blast himself. He saved at least two of his fellow marines. Dunham died from his wounds several days later.

Marines in Office

After leaving the military, many marines continue to serve the United States in political offices. Mike Coffman joined the USMC in 1979. He returned to active duty in 2005 to serve in Iraq, leaving his position as Colorado state treasurer. He is now a Colorado congressman.

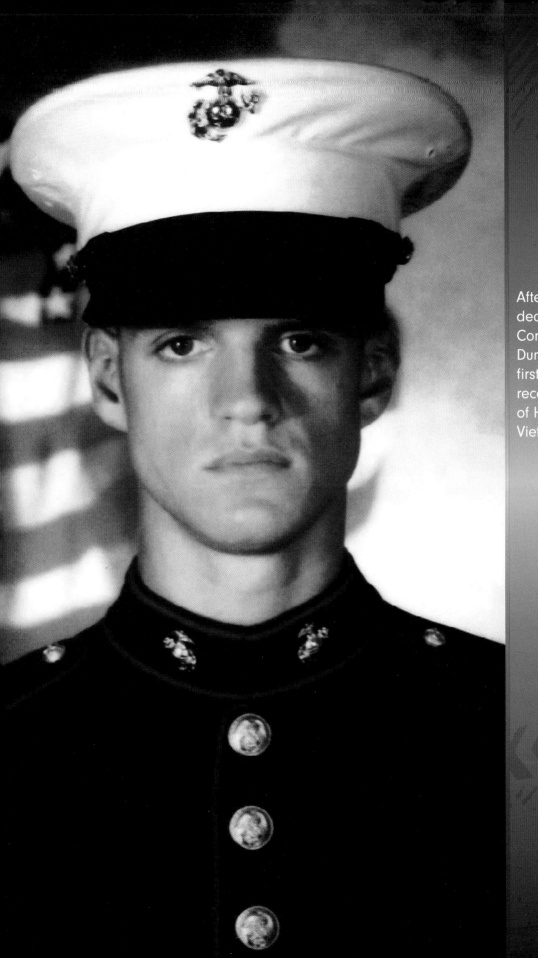

After his heroic death in Iraq, Corporal Jason Dunham was the first marine to receive the Medal of Honor since the Vietnam War.

The support center for wounded marines and their families was renamed the Sergeant Merlin German Wounded Warrior Call Center in 2008 to honor German.

United States Marine Corps

Sergeant Merlin German
Wounded Warrior Call Center
This plaque stands as a lasting tribute
to the bravery and fighting spirit to
a true warrior and defender of freedom.
Sgt Merlin German, USMC
1985 – 2008

Dedication this 4th day of December 2008

A US marine sergeant became a hero to many after he survived a roadside bomb in Iraq in 2005. Sergeant Merlin German had burns covering 97 percent of his body from the explosion. German earned the nickname "Miracle Man" as he bravely worked through his injuries. He had many surgeries and learned how to walk again. Ever the determined marine, German even started a charity while he recovered in the hospital. Merlin's Miracles helps children who have been badly burned.

In 2008, German died at age 22. His memory lives on in Merlin's Miracles, which is now run by his family and friends.

Marine Movie Heroes

Because members of the USMC often perform risky missions, many movies have been made about marines and their operations. Some of these films focus on historic events, such as the World War II movie *The Halls of Montezuma*. Others, such as *Battle: Los Angeles* and *Independence Day*, feature marines saving the world from aliens!

Will Smith, center, and his family attend the opening of *Independence Day*. Smith plays a USMC captain in the movie.

FEATS OF COURAGE

Whether or not they wear a medal for bravery, all marines who serve in the USMC are heroes. They march across open plains although they know snipers have been shooting US soldiers. They run into enemy gunfire to save their fellow soldiers. Even in training, they perform tasks that require bravery, such as standing in rooms filling with **tear gas** to learn how to use gas masks.

The Marine Seal

Every US marine uniform bears the USMC seal. A gold eagle rests atop the globe, surrounded by an anchor. The background is red since red and gold are the colors of the marines. The seal serves as a reminder of the marines' goal to protect people all over the world.

Since 1775, US marines have protected the United States and other nations around the world. The next time you meet a US marine, say thank you!

Marines from the 11th Marine Expeditionary Unit arrive in Kuwait in 2010 in a CH-46 Sea Knight helicopter.

GLOSSARY

casualty: a military person killed or injured in war

combat: armed fighting between opposing forces. Also, to fight against someone or something.

corps: a group of soldiers trained for special service

draft: to select for required military service

insurgent: a person who goes against a government or group in power

Korean War: a conflict between North and South Korea that began in 1950 and ended in 1953 in which the United States joined with South Korea

mission: a task or job a group must perform

reconnaissance: the exploration of a place to collect information

recruit: a new member of a military force

sniper: a soldier specially trained to shoot well from a hiding place

tear gas: a gas released as a weapon, which causes the skin and eyes to burn

terrorist: someone who uses violence and fear to challenge an authority

Vietnam War: a conflict starting in 1955 and ending in 1975 between South Vietnam and North Vietnam in which the United States joined with South Vietnam

FOR MORE INFORMATION

Books

Payment, Simone. *Frontline Marines: Fighting in the Marine Combat Arms Units.* New York, NY: Rosen Publishing, 2007.

Reed, Jennifer. *The U.S. Marine Corps.* Mankato, MN: Capstone Press, 2009.

Schwartz, Heather. *Women of the U.S. Marine Corps: Breaking Barriers.* Mankato, MN: Capstone Press, 2011.

Websites

Congressional Medal of Honor Society
www.cmohs.org/medal-history
Learn the history of the highest award in the US military.

Marines
www.marines.mil
Read more about recent missions of the US Marine Corps.

Navy & Marine Corps Awards and Decorations
usmilitary.about.com/od/navy/l/blnavawards.htm
See pictures of many military decorations and read the history of each.

INDEX